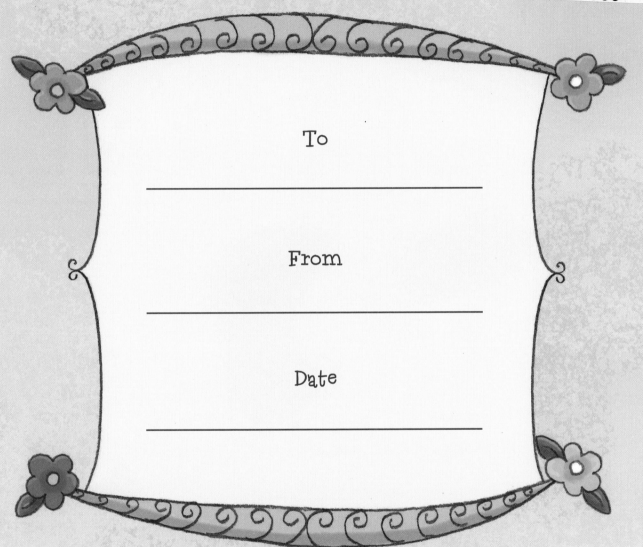

To

From

Date

Come into My Heart, Lord Jesus

Stormie Omartian
Artwork by Shari Warren

HARVEST HOUSE PUBLISHERS
EUGENE, OREGON

It's never too soon to lead a child to Jesus.

Stormie Omartian

Come into My Heart, Lord Jesus

Text Copyright © 2009 by Stormie Omartian
Art Copyright © 2013 by Shari Warren
Published by Harvest House Publishers
Eugene, Oregon 97402
www.harvesthousepublishers.com

ISBN: 978-0-7369-5068-8

Design and production by Mary pat Design, Westport, Connecticut

Select text is adapted from The Prayer That Makes God Smile by Stormie Omartian, copyright © 2009

Printed in China

13 14 15 16 17 18 19 /LP/ 10 9 8 7 6 5 4 3 2

Jesus said,
"Let the little children come to Me and do not forbid them."
Matthew 19:14

You make God happy. That's because **He loves you.** God loves you when you are **happy,**

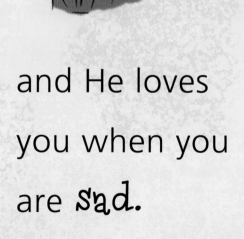

and He loves you when you are **sad.**

God loves you when you are **sleeping,**

and He loves you when you are **awake.**

There is never a time when God does not love you.

God loves you so much that He always listens to you when you talk to Him. Talking to God is called praying. He loves it when you talk to Him. Your prayers make God happy.

It makes God happy to hear all of your prayers. But there is one prayer that God loves the most. And that is the prayer you pray when you ask Jesus to come into your heart. This is the prayer that makes God smile.

God loves you so much that He **sent His Son, Jesus,** to earth to save you. That's why He is called your **Savior.** Jesus saves you from bad things and bad people. But most important of all, **He saves you** from ever having to be separated from God.

When you **receive Jesus,** it means that someday you will go to heaven and **live with God.** Jesus said that the only way to get to **heaven** is by receiving Him into our hearts first. We can't find the way without Jesus.

Heaven is a wonderful place. In heaven, you will never get sick and you will never be hurt. In heaven, there are no bad people and nothing scary ever happens. That means you won't ever be afraid or sad. In heaven, you will be happy all the time.

God wants you to be in heaven
with Him one day.
That's why He sent
Jesus to help
you get there.
But **Jesus**
doesn't just help you get
to heaven. He **helps**
you in every way **here**
on earth.

Jesus helps you by being with you all of the time. **He helps you** by listening to you and **answering your prayers.** He helps you by giving you everything you need. He helps you by making you well when you are sick and protecting you when you are in danger. That's why Jesus is **God's greatest gift** to all of us.

Jesus is the most important name in the world. Once you invite Jesus into your heart, you can call His name and He will be right there beside you.

You can't see the air, but you know it is there because you are breathing it. You can't see Jesus, but you know He is there because He has promised to be with you forever, and He never breaks His promise. Just as the air is always there keeping you alive, Jesus is always there giving you life too.

When **you pray** to receive Jesus into your heart, you become one of **God's special kids.** He is your **friend forever,** and you can **talk to Him** whenever you want.

If something goes wrong, you can tell Him about it and He will help you. If you feel sad, you can share that with Him and He will help you feel happy again. And when you are having a good day, He will help you do things for other people that make them feel good too.

Jesus said that those who **believe in Him** will have their names written in a big book in heaven called the **Book of Life.** He said we should be very happy about that. When you receive Jesus **into your heart,** your name will be written in that big book too.

You get to **make choices** every day. You choose which toy **to play** with or which story **to read.** You choose the words **you speak** and many of the things **you do.** Receiving Jesus into your heart is also a choice you get to make. Jesus wants you to **choose to receive Him.** You get to decide when and where.

When you are ready to receive Jesus into your heart, you can say the prayer on the last page. You only have to say it once if you really mean it. After you pray this prayer, write your name on the line and put in the date. That way you will always remember when you said the prayer that makes God smile. And it will remind you that your name is written in God's big book in heaven.

My Prayer to Receive Jesus

"Dear Jesus, I believe You are God's Son. Please come into my heart to live. Forgive me for anything I have ever done wrong. Thank You that someday I will live in heaven with You. Thank You that You love me and will always take care of me. I love You too."

My name is_____.

I said this prayer and meant it on this day

_____

and this year _____ .